anythink

D0772651

JUNIOR GEOLOGIST
Discovering Rocks, Minerals, and Gems

WHAT ARE GEMS?

BOBI MARTIN

Britannica®
Educational Publishing

IN ASSOCIATION WITH

ROSEN
EDUCATIONAL SERVICES

Published in 2016 by Britannica Educational Publishing (a trademark of Encyclopædia Britannica, Inc.) in association with The Rosen Publishing Group, Inc.
29 East 21st Street, New York, NY 10010

Distributed exclusively by Rosen Publishing.
To see additional Britannica Educational Publishing titles, go to rosenpublishing.com.

First Edition

Britannica Educational Publishing
J.E. Luebering: Director, Core Reference Group
Mary Rose McCudden: Editor, Britannica Student Encyclopedia

Rosen Publishing
Shalini Saxena: Editor
Nelson Sá: Art Director
Nicole Russo: Designer
Cindy Reiman: Photography Manager
Nicole Baker: Photo Researcher

Library of Congress Cataloging-in-Publication Data

Martin, Bobi, author.
 What are gems? / Bobi Martin. — First edition.
   pages cm. — (Junior geologist : discovering rocks, minerals, and gems)
 Audience: Grades 1-4.
 Includes bibliographical references and index.
 ISBN 978-1-68048-245-4 (library bound) — ISBN 978-1-5081-0050-8 (pbk.) — ISBN 978-1-68048-303-1 (6-pack)
 1. Gems—Juvenile literature. 2. Crystals–Juvenile literature. I. Title.
 QE392.2.M37 2016
 553.8–dc23
                                                                                                    2015016297
Manufactured in the United States of America

Photo credits: Cover, p. 1 J. Palys/Shutterstock.com; cover and interior pages background Elnur/Shutterstock.com; p. 4 De Agostini/A. Rizzi/Getty Images; p. 5 Tim Graham/Getty Images; p. 6 © Steve Estvanik/Fotolia; p. 7 Michael Mauney/The LIFE Picture Collection/Getty Images; p. 8 Chris Ralph; p. 9 MvH/E+/Getty Images; pp. 10, 20 Encyclopaedia Britannica, Inc.; p. 11 Robert D Pinna/Shutterstock.com; p. 12 Luis Davilla/Cover/Getty Images; p. 13 Howard Grey/The Image Bank/Getty Images; p. 14 Yves Gellie/Gamma-Rapho/Getty Images; p. 15 Bloomberg/Getty Images; p. 16 © iStockphoto.com/bratan007; pp. 17, 18 Joel Arem/Science Source/Getty Images; p. 19 Peter Macdiarmid/Getty Images; p. 21 Andreas Koschate/Getty Images; p. 22 Mike Dabell/E+/Getty Images; p. 23 Visuals Unlimited, Inc./GIPhotoStock/Getty Images; p. 24 Print Collector/Hulton Archive/Getty Images; p. 25 Robbie George/National Geographic Image Collection/Getty Images; p. 26 © Leemage/Bridgeman Images; p. 27 kornilov007/Shutterstock.com; p. 28 Carlo Bevilacqua/Scala/Art Resource, New York; p. 29 Ron Levine/Digital Vision/Getty Images; interior pages (arrow) Mushakesa/Shutterstock.com.

CONTENTS

GLITTERY GEMS

People around the world have loved gems for thousands of years. We prize them for their beautiful colors and for their rarity. The more difficult it is to find a gem, the more valuable it usually is. Some of the most valued gems are rubies, emeralds, sapphires, and diamonds.

In the past, most gemstones cost so much that only royalty could afford them.

Gemstones come in many different colors, sizes, shapes, and cuts. Sizes and shapes vary depending on how the gem will be used.

The Crown Jewels of England are displayed in a museum inside the Tower of London.

Today, almost everyone can own gems of some kind. Gifts of jewelry with gemstones are often given as a sign of affection. For example, diamonds are used in most engagement and wedding rings. Some gems are thought to bring good health or good luck, while others are said to be unlucky or even cursed! Some famous gemstones are displayed in museums so that everyone can enjoy them.

Think About It

In the past, only wealthy people could afford to buy gems. Do you think this made gems more appealing? Why or why not?

HOW DO GEMS FORM?

Most gems are minerals, which are natural substances found in the ground. There are many minerals, but only certain kinds are beautiful and strong enough to be gems. Some gems are created by heat. Deep under the surface of Earth, a very hot substance called magma is always moving. When magma pushes up between layers of rock, it mixes with different minerals. As the magma cools, different types of gems can form.

Other gems are formed deep inside Earth. The upper layers of Earth constantly press on the

Obsidian forms from lava or magma that cools quickly. Obsidian gems have been used for many purposes.

lower layers. Where minerals are present, this pressure, along with heat from inside Earth, creates gems. Some gems form from evaporating water, or water that is heated and turns to gas. Water near Earth's

Turquoise is formed when water dissolves minerals in certain types of rock.

surface dissolves minerals it comes into contact with. As that water evaporates, gems can form and be left behind.

Compare and Contrast

Compare and contrast the different ways gems are formed. What do all gems have in common?

SOME MINERALS MAKE MANY GEMSTONES

Gems are formed in many different ways. A mineral can mix with different natural elements such as iron or copper. When this happens, some minerals can form more than one type of gemstone. For example, beryl is a colorless mineral. But when it mixes with chromium, green emeralds form. Mixed with iron, beryl creates blue aquamarines, and a rose-colored morganite comes from the presence of manganese.

Morganite (*left*), aquamarine (*middle*), and heliodor (*right*) are three different varieties of beryl.

Another mineral that makes more than one type of gemstone is corundum. When corundum has traces of copper, iron, or titanium, it forms blue, green, purple, pink, or yellow sapphires. Corundum mixed with chromium becomes rubies. Quartz is one of the most common minerals. Gems that come from quartz include purple amethyst, yellow citrine, and many others.

Amethyst ranges from pale lavender to deep purple. Quartz forms gems of other colors, too.

Compare and Contrast

Compare the way the element chromium turns the minerals beryl and corundum into gems. How are the gems similar? How are they different?

CRYSTALS

Diamonds, emeralds, and many other gems are also crystals. A crystal is a type of solid object. Matter is made up of tiny particles called atoms. Atoms combine to form molecules. If the molecules are arranged in a regular pattern that repeats itself, then the object is a crystal. Not all solid objects are crystals. Glass is solid, but its molecules are not arranged in a pattern so it is not a crystal.

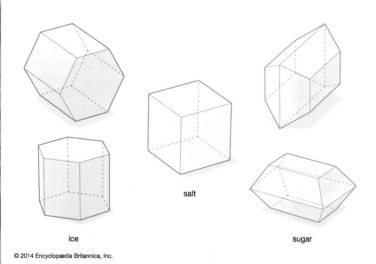

salt

ice

sugar

© 2014 Encyclopædia Britannica, Inc.

Different substances have different crystal shapes. But all crystals of the same substance have the same shape.

The way an object's molecules are joined together creates the crystal's shape. On the outside, crystals have flat sides that meet in sharp corners. Crystals can form many different shapes, but all crystals of the same substance will have the same pattern. For example, no matter what color they are, all quartz crystals have six-sided columns.

Think About It

Crystals have many different shapes and patterns. How do you think this affects the way different gems look?

Gem-quality quartz may be clear, pink, violet, or other colors. But all colors of quartz have six-sided columns.

GEMS FROM PLANTS AND ANIMALS

Not all gems are minerals. A few are created by animals or plants. These are called organic gems. Pearls are formed inside mollusks such as oysters, mussels, and clams. Sometimes a grain of sand or another irritant gets between the mollusk's body and its shell. The animal coats the bothersome bit with a smooth substance called nacre. After many years, the layers of nacre build up and form a pearl.

Pearls can grow inside any mollusk but are most often found in oysters.

Coral is a gem that comes from the skeletons of tiny sea animals. Coral can be red, pink, black, white, or blue.

Some gems come from plant substances. Amber is tree resin that has hardened over many years. Most amber is yellowish and is transparent, or see-through. Sometimes insects or bits of plants became trapped in the resin before it hardened. Amber that includes such fossilized pieces is more valuable than plain amber.

Pieces of amber that include fossilized insects or plants may be valued at thousands of dollars.

SYNTHETIC GEMS

Natural gems take thousands of years to form. They can be hard to find and expensive to mine from the ground. Since the 1800s, people have looked for ways to make gems more quickly. Synthetic gems are made in a laboratory using the same minerals as natural gems. Scientists mix mineral solutions and then put them into heated machines.

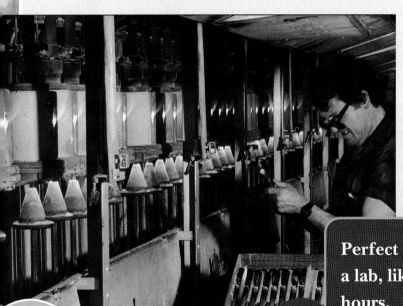

Instead of taking years, these crystals are large enough to be cut and polished in just a few days. They look like gems that

Perfect rubies can be created in a lab, like this one, in just a few hours.

These rough diamonds were grown in a lab. They are just like rough diamonds in nature.

are found in nature because they are made from the same minerals. Even many jewelers cannot tell the difference between naturally grown gems and high-quality synthetic gems. It takes a trained expert to tell them apart.

Compare and Contrast

Both natural gems and synthetic gems are beautiful. In what other ways are they the same? How are they different?

IDENTIFYING GEMSTONES

It is difficult to identify gemstones by color alone. Some gems, like turquoise or rubies, come in shades of just one color. But others—like quartz, tourmaline, and sapphires—come in many colors, including clear. Diamonds can be clear, yellow, pink, blue, or black! And several different kinds of gems can be almost the same color. For example, garnets, sapphires, and emeralds can be green. Some aquamarine and topaz gems are similar shades of light blue.

↑ Most diamonds are clear, like the one on the right. But diamonds come in many other colors, too.

Hematite (*left*) always leaves a reddish streak on porcelain. Malachite (*right*) leaves a green streak.

Experts use many tests to identify gems properly. Streak is a simple, but helpful, test. When a mineral is rubbed against a piece of rough, unglazed porcelain, the color of the powder it leaves is called its streak. Even when two pieces of the same gemstone are different colors, they will usually leave the same color of streak.

Think About It

Minerals that grow in different colors can be tricky to identify. How does knowing about streak help experts identify gemstones?

MOHS SCALE OF HARDNESS

Rating the hardness of a mineral helps identify it. In 1812, Friedrich Mohs, a mineralogist, developed a hardness scale that is still used today. Mohs chose 10 common minerals all mineralogists would know. The scale goes from softest to hardest. Talc, the softest mineral, is number 1 on the scale. Diamond, the hardest mineral, is number 10.

Minerals with low numbers on the scale are more easily scratched than minerals with high numbers. Harder gemstone minerals are therefore not as likely to be scratched when worn as jewelry. For example, rubies

Harder materials scratch materials that are softer. The scratch test determines how hard a mineral is.

Rubies and diamonds are durable gems that work well in jewelry. This set was worn by a duchess in England.

and sapphires are a 9 on the Mohs scale, which means they are very durable. But amber is a 2, which means it is easily scratched. Gemstones with a score of 7 and above are usually the best choices for jewelry.

Vocabulary

A *mineralogist* is a scientist who studies and classifies minerals.

GEMS SPARKLE IN JEWELRY

Uncut gems often look like plain rocks or bits of glass. In the 1400s, people discovered how to cut transparent gems to give them many flat surfaces called facets. Transparent gems like topaz and rubies have facets that reflect more light and help these gems sparkle. Gems such as jade and turquoise are opaque, which means you cannot see through them. Opaque gems are usually cut with a smooth, domed surface and a flat bottom. Then they are polished to create a shine. How well a gemstone has been cut can determine the value of the stone.

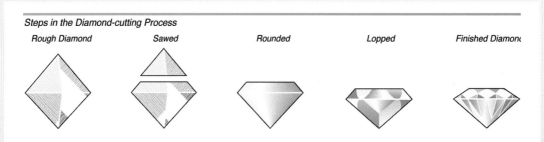

Steps in the Diamond-cutting Process

Rough Diamond   Sawed   Rounded   Lopped   Finished Diamond

Gems like diamonds are cut and shaped with special saws, cutters, and grinders so they sparkle.

Transparent gems are measured in carats, which is a unit of weight, not size. This can be confusing since a heavier gem may be smaller in size than another gem that is lighter in weight. One carat weighs 200 milligrams, or about 0.007 ounce. Opaque gems such as pearls and opals can also be measured by size, in addition to carats.

Diamonds and other transparent gems are measured by their weight in units called carats.

Compare and Contrast

Size and weight are two ways to measure something. When would you want to use weight? When would size be better?

GEMS AT WORK

Most natural transparent gems have small flaws of some type. The smaller the flaw, the better clarity a gem has. Gems with flaws are not good for jewelry, but they can be used in other ways. For example, because they are so hard, diamonds are used to

Vocabulary

Clarity is the quality or state of being clear.

Diamonds can cut through almost anything. Diamond dust is often used to make saw blades sharp.

make sawblades, drills, and grinding tools. Diamonds are also used to make the fine blades of scalpels used by some surgeons. Sapphires are used in scientific instruments, while their common mineral, corundum, is used to make sandpaper.

Beryl, the mineral that makes emeralds, is the source of beryllium. It is used in many different things such as weather monitors and air bags. Quartz crystals are used in watches, computers, and other electronics. Quartz sand is used to make glass.

FAMOUS GEMS

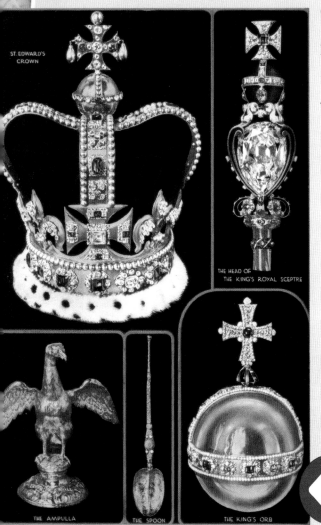

ST. EDWARD'S CROWN

THE HEAD OF THE KING'S ROYAL SCEPTRE

THE AMPULLA

THE SPOON

THE KING'S ORB

The largest diamond ever found was the Cullinan. It weighed 3,106 carats, which is more than one pound! It was cut into nine large diamonds and many smaller ones. The largest of those is sometimes called the Great Star of Africa. The huge pear-shaped diamond was set into the royal scepter, which is part of the Crown Jewels of England. This famous gem

The Crown Jewels of Britain are adorned with many expensive gems.

collection includes several crowns, scepters, swords, and other gem-studded items. Another well-known piece in the collection is the Koh-i-noor diamond, which came from India. The Crown Jewels are displayed in the Tower of London in England.

The Hope diamond is another famous gem. This dark blue diamond has been bought, stolen, and recut many times since it was discovered in the 1600s. It was donated to the Smithsonian Institute in 1958 and is on display in Washington, D.C., where everyone can admire it.

The dark blue Hope diamond is encircled by many clear diamonds. This gem is rumored to be cursed.

SUPERSTITIONS ABOUT GEMS

Over the years, people have had many superstitions about gemstones. People once ground some gems into powder and used them as medicine. For example, topaz was said to ease arthritis pain. Some people carried stones for protection. Emeralds were said to blind snakes, and tiger's eye would bring good luck.

Aaron, the first high priest of the Israelites, wore a breastplate with 12 gemstones.

Birthstones have been popular in jewelry for thousands of years. Why do you think this is?

The belief that some gemstones' power was strongest in a certain month probably came from the Bible. One of the books of the Bible describes the breastplate of the high priest Aaron as having 12 gemstones, one for each tribe of Israel. Later, many of those same gemstones were assigned to specific months of the calendar. Birthstones are still popular in jewelry today.

Many people like to wear a piece of jewelry with their birthstone. Some believe this brings good luck.

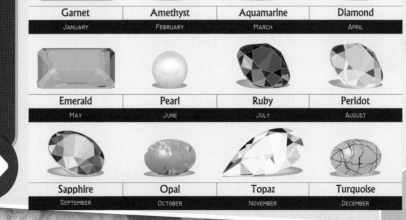

Garnet	Amethyst	Aquamarine	Diamond
JANUARY	FEBRUARY	MARCH	APRIL
Emerald	Pearl	Ruby	Peridot
MAY	JUNE	JULY	AUGUST
Sapphire	Opal	Topaz	Turquoise
SEPTEMBER	OCTOBER	NOVEMBER	DECEMBER

GEMSTONES FOR ALL AGES

Queen Elizabeth I of England wore rings, earrings, and necklaces made with gems.

People have been making and wearing jewelry for thousands of years. Throughout time, the most favored pieces of jewelry have been those with gemstones. In the Middle Ages, people shaped and polished gems to make them round and shiny. Later, people discovered how to cut transparent gems to create facets that made gems sparkle.

Our fascination with gems led to learning how to make synthetic gems. Along with gemstones that are too flawed for jewelry use, synthetic gems are used for tools, electronics, medicine, and even space equipment. Our interest in gems never gets old. Newer gems, such as tanzanite, and new colors of older gems, such as the neon-blue Paraiba tourmaline, continue to be discovered. From young to old, and from royalty to everyday people, almost everyone is fascinated with gemstones.

Compare and Contrast

Compare the way people felt about gems in the past with how we value them today. What things are different?

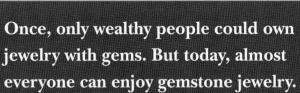

Once, only wealthy people could own jewelry with gems. But today, almost everyone can enjoy gemstone jewelry.

GLOSSARY

atom The basic building block of all matter.

crown jewels Special items usually decorated with expensive gems that are used or worn by royalty.

crystal Matter that consists of atoms and molecules arranged in a regular pattern.

durable Strong and long-lasting.

facet Flat, polished surface on a gemstone.

flaw A small imperfection that is often hidden.

irritant Something that bothers or causes annoyance.

magma Hot liquid rock found deep under Earth's surface.

mineral A substance that occurs naturally and does not come from a plant or an animal.

molecule The smallest particle of a substance that has all of the characteristics of that substance.

nacre A smooth substance mollusks use to coat foreign objects that get inside their shells.

opaque Not allowing light to shine through.

organic Made from or related to a living thing.

porcelain A hard, white ceramic material.

rarity The quality of being difficult to find.

resin A thick liquid substance that comes from trees.

superstition A belief not based on anything proven. Also, a belief based on fear or trust in magic.

synthetic Something that is produced chemically, rather than made by nature.

titanium A silvery metallic element found in nature. It is strong and lightweight.

FOR MORE INFORMATION

BOOKS

Hoffman, Steven M. *Gems, Crystals, and Precious Rocks.* New York, NY: PowerKids Press, 2011.

Owen, Ruth. *Jewelry.* New York, NY: PowerKids Press, 2013.

Peterson, Christine. *Groovy Gems.* Edina, MN: ABDO Publishing, 2010.

Squire, Ann O. *Gemstones.* New York, NY: Children's Press, 2013.

Vandenbosch, Vera. *Friendship Bracelets.* Newton, CT: Taunton Press, Inc., 2015.

Zoehfeld, Kathleen Weidner. *Rocks and Minerals.* Washington, DC: National Geographic Society, 2012.

WEBSITES

Because of the changing nature of Internet links, Rosen Publishing has developed an online list of websites related to the subject of this book. This site is updated regularly. Please use this link to access this list:

http://www.rosenlinks.com/GEOL/Gems

INDEX